Historical Etchings

Home Life

Copyright-free illustrations for lovers of history

Compiled by
Bobbie Kalman

 Crabtree Publishing Company

Historical Etchings Series

In 19th-century North America, hundreds of artists produced black-and-white steel-plate and woodcut engravings for newspapers, periodicals, books, and catalogs. Over a period of more than five years, Bobbie Kalman and Peter Crabtree traveled to libraries throughout North America to research these etchings for Crabtree Publishing Company's *Early Settler Life* series. Researching etchings meant working in climate-controlled rooms to make sure the pages of the old newspapers and books in which these etchings appeared did not crumble due to age and dryness. Special photographers had to be hired and approved.

Many of the etchings in the *Early Settler Life* series have never appeared in other collections, so Bobbie is often asked for permission to use them. By popular demand, they have been gathered into a series of their own: the *Historical Etchings* series. Today, although many of the original sources and creators' names are forgotten, these illustrations offer a fascinating glimpse into the daily lives of the settlers of North America.

Crabtree Publishing Company

350 Fifth Avenue	360 York Road, RR 4	73 Lime Walk
Suite 3308	Niagara-on-the-Lake	Headington
New York	Ontario, Canada	Oxford OX3 7AD
N.Y. 10118	L0S 1J0	United Kingdom

Cataloging in Publication Data

Kalman, Bobbie
   Home life: copyright-free illustrations for lovers of history

(Historical etchings)

ISBN 0-86505-913-6 (pbk.)
This book contains etchings and accompanying text depicting various aspects of settler home life, including hygiene, children, and the roles of women.

1. Home—North America—History—Juvenile literature.
2. Family—North America—History—Juvenile literature.
I. Title. II. Series: Kalman, Bobbie. Historical etchings.

HQ535.H583 1997   j306'.09   LC 97-39756
                                                CIP

Contents

Living in the wilderness was a lonely experience. The new settlers missed the family and friends they left behind in the "Old Country." Their new neighbors were miles away.

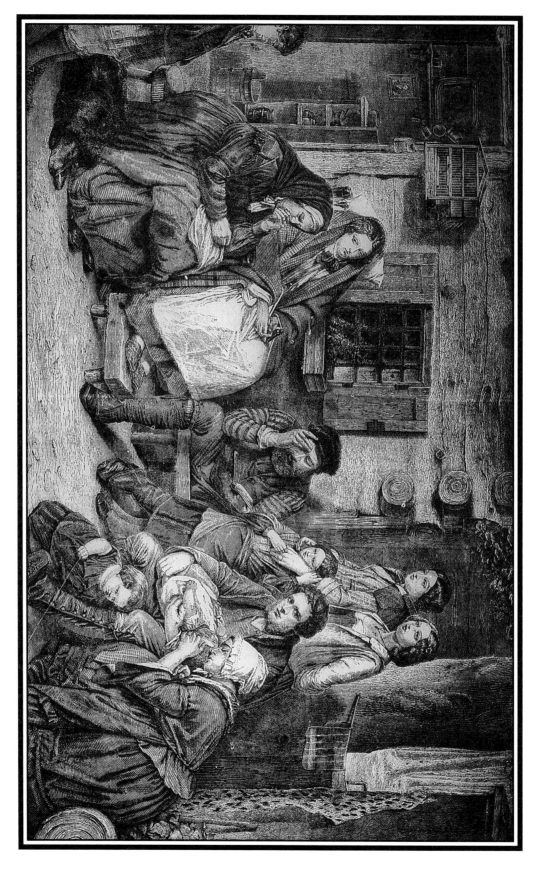

On special occasions, neighbors would come from miles around to eat, drink, dance, and socialize. Parties such as this one helped relieve some of the loneliness of life in the New World.

Dinner was cooked in huge iron pots that hung over the fire. Women had to be careful that their dress didn't catch fire while they were cooking.

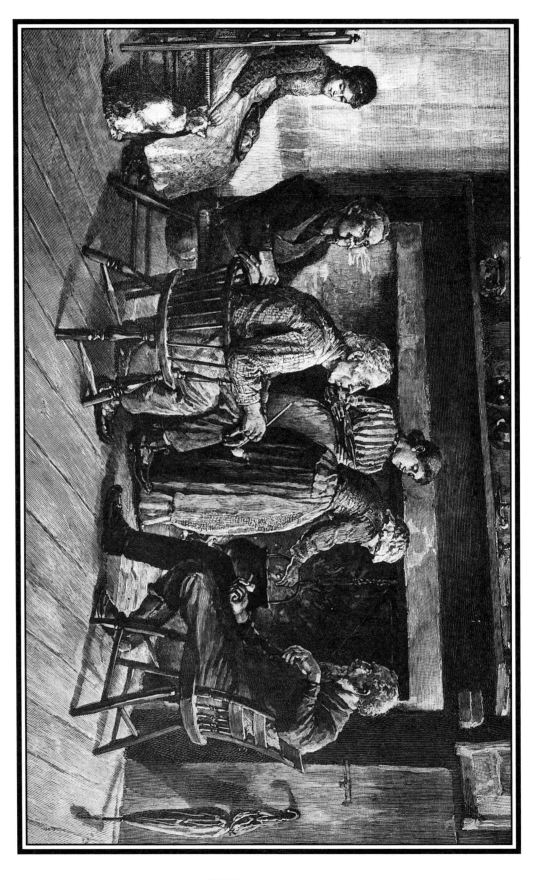

Preparing Thanksgiving dinner was a job for the whole family. Grandfather weighs the turkey. Grandmother and mother are ready to stuff it and put it in the bake oven. Sister shells peas while brother mixes batter for the cake that mother will bake.

Besides cooking, many kinds of work were done in the kitchen. By the light of the fire, mother spun wool into yarn on a spinning wheel. She now uses the pegs on the wall to wind skeins of yarn.

While their grandchildren sleep, these grandparents make toys for them. Christmas is just around the corner!

Children often made up their own games for entertainment. Building a card house was a simple pleasure for children lucky enough to have a deck of playing cards.

Children loved pretending to do the work of the adults around them. These children are practicing to become doctors, apothecaries, apprentices, and future patients!

Fathers taught their sons to follow in their footsteps. This fisherman is showing his young son how to make a fishing net.

This father is a lobster fisherman. There are no schools where he and his son live, so when the weather is too rough for fishing, he teaches his son to read.

Many young girls did not go to school. They stayed at home and helped their mothers with the cooking, cleaning, sewing, and care of their younger brothers and sisters.

Sewing, knitting, and crocheting were a part of every girl's education. Parents believed their daughters needed to learn these home crafts in order to become good wives and mothers.

This grandmother is teaching her granddaughter how to read at home. Many girls did not have the opportunity to go to school.

Playing the piano was part of a wealthy girl's education. This daughter enjoys her mother's music and hopes to play as well someday.

The kitchen fireplace was the main source of light in the evenings. In other parts of the house, people used candles to light their way.

People did not have indoor plumbing until the late 1800s. They got their water from a well. Water was brought up from the well by pumping a handle.

Rainwater was collected in barrels that were placed under a downspout from the roof. Rainwater was "soft," so it was ideal for washing hair and clothes. It was also good drinking water.

People did not bathe very often because they were worried they would lose their body oils. They believed these oils kept them from getting sick. This boy does not care about body oils—he just doesn't like bathing!

There were no bathrooms, so men shaved in their bedroom. They used a shaving mug, brush, and straight razor.

Instead of washing hair often, as people do today, girls and women brushed their hair 100 strokes a day. Most girls needed help brushing their long hair.

When a husband died, a wife had no way of supporting herself or her children. Many widows and their children were very poor.

Women spent their days cooking and cleaning. In those days, few women worked outside the home. They did not have a chance to have careers.

One of the few jobs available to women in the nineteenth century was cleaning other people's homes. Young girls who came from Europe worked as maids for wealthy people.

House servants had many jobs to do. If they made a mistake, they were punished. In many homes, even the children were allowed to boss around the servants.

Most wealthy girls were not taught to cook by their mother. They took lessons so that, once they were married, they could run a kitchen and give instructions to their servants.

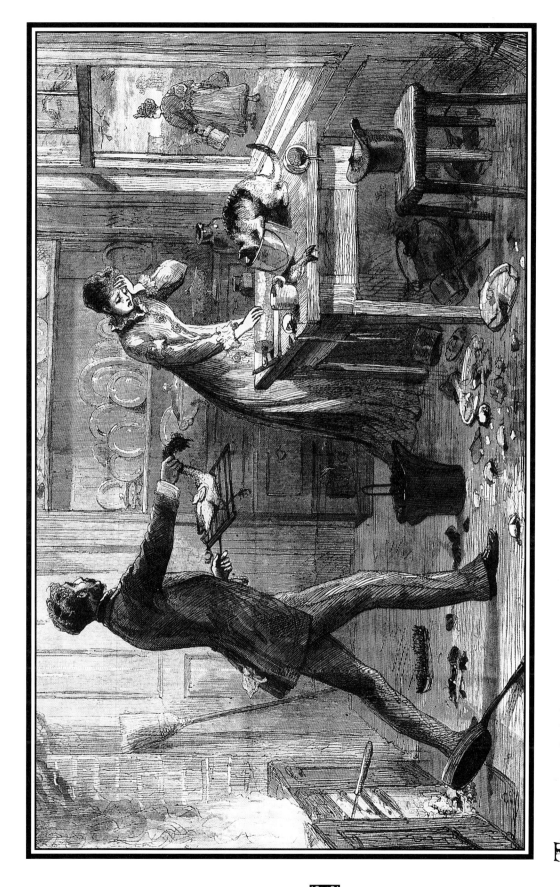

This young wife did not take cooking lessons. Now she is in trouble because her servant has quit. Her husband is very unhappy about the cooking, but the cat seems to like it!

While her husband reads his newspaper, this young wife feeds the children under the watchful eye of her mother-in-law. Nineteenth-century women had very few rights. They were expected to keep their husbands and children happy.

Young wives cared for the children and kept house without the help of their husband. Husbands felt that the home was their place to relax and forget about work. This woman wishes her husband would look after their daughter for once!

Hosts and guests were required to follow a rigid dining etiquette or risk offending others. This young man has angered his host by refusing to say grace before the meal.